dancing letters

Dawnbreaker Poetry Series

Dancing Letters by Miguel Cruz
Christmas Poetry by J. E. Deegan
In Search of Moonlit Crevices by Marcel Wormsley

~ ~ ~

For a full catalog of works by Miguel Cruz
and other authors, please visit
dawnbreakerpress.com

dancing letters

Miguel Cruz

Dawnbreaker Press

Galveston, Texas

Designed by Chandler Barton
Illustrated by Catherine Stroud

Published by
Dawnbreaker Press
Galveston, Texas
dawnbreakerpress.com

For information, direct sales, and all other inquiries,
please email web@dawnbreakerpress.com

ISBN-13:
978-0-9992054-1-9 (paperback)
978-0-9992054-2-6 (hardcover)

Also available as an e-book

First edition, 2018

Typeset in Goudy Old Style

i turn my pages
and find you
every person i meet is a letter
or a space between pretty words
proving life is a story
i met someone who made a sentence
then a chapter
now a book

girl with the broken wings
kissed by fire and loved by me
hold dear the sweet memory
our first night
the night i got so close you began to cry
lost words and in time
in love
in love with me

it's true i don't lie
i lie with just you
the salty tears that pour from those blue eyes
beautiful tears
maybe stars
no
just beautiful

beautiful girl
they cry for you
the rain pours so you can dance
drink the poison from above
love without thought
love because you can
love because you don't know
love because you are afraid you'll never feel this way again

i'm brave to write
late at night
with you in sight
brave to love someone i can never deserve

i'll rip my wings so you can fly
fly away
far away
to a world that you deserve

Miguel Cruz

withering away to become so fragile
torn from depths of oneself
ration of consequences omitted in hollow
perfection the fragmentation of a damned soul
beating to predestined creation
molded from blind perception
graceful of the blackened cavity
invitation to the acceptance of spoken truth

you hiccup when you eat
you can chew popcorn the rest of your life
you grind your teeth at night
and if you don't sleep you get sick
you tickle everywhere
that's your weakness
you are clumsy
and fall on your two left feet
yet dance with such grace
you can read a book for days
so i wrote you one
you plan every detail
you are forgiving
you enjoy the little things
hot teas
deep conversations
or a kiss on the cheek
your lower back has a scar
the shape of a moon
you get self-conscious about that
you are intelligent and creative
yet barely speak aloud
when you get overstressed you break down
and cry until you feel better
you have more freckles than there are stars
you press yourself to be perfect
too perfect
i not only love you
i know you

Miguel Cruz

4

i don't want to wake up
each day is another without you
i am filled with selfless motives
that make me seem selfish
maybe i simply am selfish
for wanting every moment of my life with you
i can't speak for how you feel
but i can think about it

soft puddles on a concrete street
raindrops tap my window
they want to come in
cold raindrops need warmth too
they fall for me
so i am not alone
countless raindrops in the storm
i will always fall for you

Miguel Cruz

i am left with as many scars as i have given
too broke to stand alone
each smile you give me
mends me whole
you do not give me old broken pieces of myself
you break yourself to give me the pieces you are

i dreamt of you again
you looked beautiful
i didn't question the reality
you weren't there
but i felt you
you spoke to me
i felt your warm breath
thorns in a rose
protect you
while red petals
wither away
i was meant to stay with you through death
protecting your soul
a lifeless rose

Miguel Cruz

your angel wings flew so high
can we can fly away
to live eternity in dreams
you and i
beauty is a burning tree
leaves the wicks for candle light
making life praise you
fly away with me

a beautiful scene of fire and me
a ballroom of burning roses
a flame dancing with a shadow
moving as one
as if they can't live with each other
the shadow is what the flame would be
the flame is what the shadow should be
the shadow makes the flame brighter
the flame makes the shadow lighter
a beautiful scene of fire and me
my love
burn for me

Miguel Cruz

she looked at me and it started
i felt loved from the beginning
a stranger who made me home
untogether now
if i find you again
with this body or my next
i will reintroduce our souls
i'd like to meet a beautiful star
even one with a pretended smile
my star's shine hurts
but the brightness
the joy
the waking up next to her
my memory still bleeds
but now my scars shine
the clouds
like her voice
visit me at night
and whisper don't go
but a star belongs in the sky

when my lily
sings songs so sad
the cloud cries rain
perfect petals torn by tears
leaves like sieves drink deeply
life spills so swiftly
we are drowning
you and me lily
my tears today
will be tomorrows rain
you will reign
sincerely on your hill

Miguel Cruz

whisper all around me
i will never tell
even beautiful flowers die
burned in sun
drowned in water
so pretty
yet here you are
beautiful

such a perfect thing in an imperfect world
with profound grief
she gently asks what is wrong with me
the world can't handle such perfection
the people you meet won't understand you
if imperfection is all that has ever been known
how can such a perfect thing walk with us
tears in her eyes
awaiting answers
i reply
i love you

Miguel Cruz

take a step back
to a picture i lived
she blows a kiss
i caught off camera
i was shot inside
call it lust
call it love
it is only you

my fingers break one by one
as i write for you
they bleed tears
i say to each one
change will come
the words will break someone
your pain will be hers
as they have been ours
break more for her
as the ink becomes blood
my fingers break one by one
because i'm in love with you

Miguel Cruz

i tend to smile at pretty things
deep connections built on the staring of eyes
a returned smile and a guess at your thoughts
games that we play for pastime
how are you this beautiful
a beautiful woman with a pearl necklace
pretty on beauty
do you hide behind the beauty
a beautiful symbol

this was never my plan
i never knew i'd meet you
i never knew i'd love you
i never knew i'd lose you
you were never my plan
but i thank God each day for you

Miguel Cruz

moon light glistens past the thin branches of the tree
leaving shadows and dew on leaves
frigid breeze and violent wind further amplifies the power of the
proud tree
sunken roots each with purpose
perfectly divided for unity
as the tree cries for the loss of leaves branches and roots
it uses the tears to strengthen itself
to grow so that they did not go in vain
an individual leaf provides shade for life
in that of itself
the simple life of a tree
to grow tall and more beautiful with age
to be tested admired and nurtured
a home for many
a peaceful memory
the seed of life
many trees in our world each with their own name
yet all with different purposes
a story within a story
for in my story i am a star
looking below at the moon and trees
in yours i may be a simple background
the insignificance of dirt on the road
you pay no mind to me
yet i to you
for trees listen
who am i
the star who looks from up above
the tree dancing in the wind
the moon who provides the light at night
or the dirt on the road who you look past
i will be the dirt on the road
who will be carried through the wind
embracing a tree one day providing nourishment and growth
so the tree may grow closer to the moon light
and with the years it will grow closer to the stars
who will one day see my significance and carry me to them
i am everything because you are my everything

dancing letters

a broken record
scratches the needle of my life
melancholy tunes
i offer the words written of a broken soul
yearning to be the reason you grow

Miguel Cruz

she broke through open doors
and brought a storm
it's never been the same

my eyes see a golden fire
feel the burning embers
made by memories
each second it dies
i add new dreams
flames rise
as it should be
if the memories are forgotten
and the dreams turn into nightmares
add me
with my burning body
we might just be

Miguel Cruz

black dress
black dress
hair in a mess
i must confess
i hate dreaming
dreaming of things
that make me sing

winter wine to bear the pain
as if that smile could kill me less
deadly and true
only to be you

Miguel Cruz

i dream of quiet nights and written thoughts
a place for you and i to be honest
each stroke of my pen a lie cannot pass
each letter scripted to paper is an unspoken bond which grows stronger
i fear the day when you read this and understand
when my candle finally dies down
the pain within grows
each sweet word spoken unknowingly
each quiet whisper from within
my soul yearns
the thing about a secret is that it will always want to be found
i secretly love you
yet i keep the secret from myself

soft spoken and kind the girl is
taking more cream than sugar in her coffee

Miguel Cruz

she sees through those who want her heart
but looks at me with her mind's eye
seas of affection

i sit with you for hours
with silence
this is we

Miguel Cruz

at storms end beneath the broken trees
lies me
washed to shore
with the wolf at night
the blood moon so oddly reassuring
with what little breath is left
i pray for that wolf
sharpening teeth with bones
still a sharper tongue

autumn leaves
on a summers winter blue
falling for me as i fell for you

Miguel Cruz

i breathe deeply
slowly realizing i'm losing my mind

the wind follows me
bright lights all around me
screaming my completion
there they go again and again
do you feel it
it's what makes me breathe the glowing air
too beautiful for words
each thought in mind
like a ripple in broken water
each curve delighted to be at the presence of life
opportunity is each breath i take
why can't i breathe at times

Miguel Cruz

i fell
but didn't fall
i levitated
flowing through my veins
a rush
that blush in your cheek
my heart beats for you
my mind thinks of you
my hand writes for you

tightly pressing your hips
gently kissing your lips
staring into my world
reminding me that i'm alone
alone with my beautiful girl

Miguel Cruz

i'm in a storm
bringing beauty in chaos
eye set on you
tear the rain
for years
the crashing waves
a melody
love is my storm

farther than the moon
and more than the stars
a promise made to me
the moon came too close
and the stars proved too few and far between
i will catch the moon and throw it back
but the stars
those few stars left
i can only pray that they return to me

Miguel Cruz

our last dance
there was no music
just tears
the beating of broken hearts
those beautiful tears
from a beautiful girl
i promise i will be here

no one will ever hurt you
i promise to protect you till the end

Miguel Cruz

i dreamed of a garden
flowers blooming a single color
it reflected your eyes
and i wished to die on something so beautiful

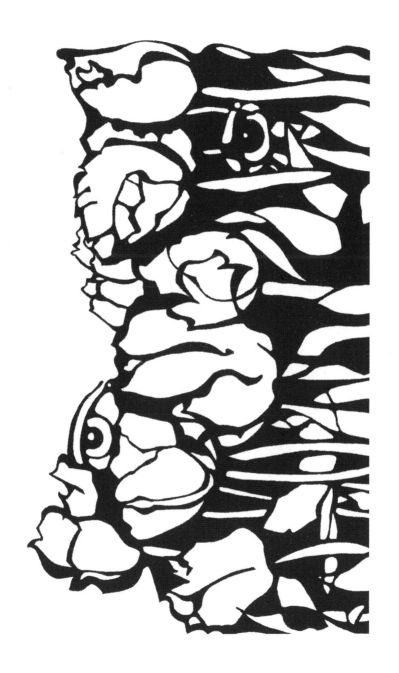

still frames delight the memory of me
was to say the least
strumming bright notes of the humming blue sky
wondering if we all think alike
she walks here
he walked there
do their paths know
i wish roads would speak

i had no words
yet i had every thought
holding you close
i felt my heart beating
each shaky breath you took
reminded me how different things would be
my best friend
gone

Miguel Cruz

thank you for the dance
the last words i said to you
each step i took felt heavy
i saw your face
the tears you cried for me
fell on the ground i walked on
but in my memories
i will always see your fire

the old man in the coffee shop is still here
the old fence by the church still stands
the old roads we walked on
i still walk on
i still think on
i still cry on
walk on these roads with me
like you once did
hold my hand
kiss my lips
say i love you
like you once did

Miguel Cruz

an oak tree fell on top of me
i forgave it
and now it grows

a dance never dies
only pausing between songs
each step i took froze time
each spin was to admire your full beauty
in our moments
i felt alive
if you forget
remember
a dance never dies

Miguel Cruz

those sleepless nights where you'd lie there
thinking at thoughts alone
a ravenous cycle
and a light sleeper
floating feathers in mind
as they caress your body
the sweet moans of the flow
i've met you once
once alone
and never left your side

if it hurts to think of you
i can't imagine seeing you
will i cry if you smile
will i stumble my words
will i have the shaky breath
will i tell you the truth

Miguel Cruz

the moon and ocean waltz
an eternal dance
a reminder of our love

silently thinking is also a lie

Miguel Cruz

i swear it rains because you cry
you hide
near the window by your book shelf
the smell of books alone gives you comfort
knowing the world
is real
real enough
to mask the pains of broken reality
each page offering you an escape
a girl with so much to offer
gives all that she has
my treasure
my beauty
my world
know in mind
a boy writes countless hours
to show you with each letter
to show you with each word
that you are worth more than
more than words on a page

Miguel Cruz

we may not be on the same page
but in the end
we are together

i can never take the pain from your bleeding heart
i can only offer my broken one
in hope that one day you'll be whole

Miguel Cruz

i was there to catch your tears
the night you felt alone
when the tears rolled down my cheeks
you held me
and let me go slowly

i would hold you without words
in your eyes what i see
a girl so broken
a girl so free
a girl made just for me

Miguel Cruz

she drinks from the broken coffee mug
and still smiles

she looks in the mirror and cries
whispering lies
my heart screams to let her know she's beautiful

my star burned me
promising she's different
yes
all so different
if you forget our love
look up and know i will be smiling

Miguel Cruz

little flower never forget to grow
those blooming petals full of color
i promise to keep you safe
never will you drown
never will you dry
just be beautiful
the seed within you so perfect
the soil beneath you full of nourishment
those thorns you grew
i would hold gently
my little flower can protect herself
if the clouds never come use my tears
use them to grow
and if the sun stops shining use my words
use them to know little flower
you are too beautiful to feel alone

you read these words knowing
that my paper is wet
thinking of you and your perfect imperfections

it wasn't a dream
that night we made love
i lifted you and our spirits rose
i laid you down gently
with each kiss down your neck
with each finger that gently caressed your frame
you knew i loved you
we whispered our secrets
our hopes
our doubts
our future
we cried in bed vulnerable
not knowing if it was right
your uncertainty was beautifully daunting
we prayed
and for a moment
that moment
everything was perfect
perfect knowing that my star came back to me

Miguel Cruz

i dance with memories
a slow dance that went by too fast

my heart feels a deep sorrow
knowing you once kissed my lips
these lips that taste of salty tears

i peel the skin off my lips
tasting the sweat on your neck
strawberry wine
i get drunk at the thought of you
a high i never leave
as the needle pierces my heart slowly
my eyes roll back
there you are
a girl who will never leave my mind
i see you dancing in the living room
care free
for me
if you could see what i see
you'd understand
a girl who deserves a man
who would break himself to make you whole
my star in the night
never lose sight
the words i write for you
for every letter is a tear i cry

Miguel Cruz

i travel at night
to seek the quiet places
the memories of you are stronger there
your black dress flowing
my tie around your neck
i squeeze gently
whispering to those memories
fade away
i can see your breath
leaving
i give you my last cold breath
in hopes that one day you'll be free

take my breath away
take it to our secret place
kiss me by the fire
hang me by the tree
hold dear the sweet words i say to you
for you never know when
my last breath is
for you never know when
my beat is gone forever
take my book
burn it by the tree
let it be a reminder that i love thee
and when my pages turn to ashes
pick them up
recreate me

Miguel Cruz

our embers burn
the flame is small
but beautiful
i hold onto the fire
even though it burns me
even though you aren't here
i see you through the flames
i pray you stay
that you grow
your tears drown you
and you wonder why
add tears to the fire
and our love will be eternal

Miguel Cruz

you hang dead leaves on your ears
who also need love
that's the beauty i see in you

she wears a blue skirt
and drinks the sweet tea from a jar
smiling at piano keys
her mind dances
a soul so free
a place where i want to be

Miguel Cruz

a kiss from you
is my life leaving

i'm reminded each day God is real
he created you

Miguel Cruz

her hair sways
as she sips from her coffee cup
awake enough to get by
are you really living
summer sweaters
and baby blue eyes that match the clouds
smiling at a screen
the slightest reflection of a beautiful dream
i wish she wished wishes true
an angel
maybe
that's not the case
just a beautiful girl
in summer blues

yearning gaze at the small hours
sensual lips the nectar of lust
curves smooth as the frame of your beauty
riding away our problems
yet we are static
sadist equal at part
yet i to blame
deeper thoughts
than i in you
throbbing pulse of conviction
you feel it too

Miguel Cruz

piano keys vibrate my heart
a series of rings and bells
the composer creates the melody
i choose to listen
the broken e flat
a little off stepped
but something altogether unique
as the keys dance on water
create hurricanes
let the water over flow
as you sink to the bottom
don't hold your breath
look around and breathe
soon you'll see that the choice you made has gotten rid of everything

i learned to live without breathing
from the moment i met you
you left me breathless
when you left me
i took a deep breath and nothing

Miguel Cruz

i can't force a dead star to shine
she looks beautiful either way

i wish you could see what i did
what i do
for you
behind closed doors i pray
when the door opens i pray
a full cup of coffee in my hand
yet they feel empty
the spaces between my fingers is where you should be
i can never drink too many
the coffee that is
but the wine eases my pain
i toast to our memories
as i pray that my hands would be filled with yours again

Miguel Cruz

i drown in wine
and inhale smoke
because the world is that beautiful

i saw your eyes
a beautiful blue reflecting the oceans mood
my emotions rush in like falling water
a blue waterfall
i jump in hoping to drown
as i lie floating
i look to the skies and see you
many forms of you
the sunrise and sunset
even the clouds have you
the birds fly in pairs
and i whisper them a secret very known
that i love you more than life
hoping to one day kiss the lips that let me go so harshly
my beautiful storm
i'm drowning for you
when i wash to shore
without breath or a beat in my chest
i would know that i fought my very best

Miguel Cruz

baby hairs in the morning
and no make up
your laughter wakes me up
with your mouth guard that helps you not grind your teeth
my big t shirt your comfy underwear
and those blue glasses you wear that complement your spirit
a beautiful girl
night and day
i say
i pray i get to wake up to my sleeping angel
that is when you are most beautiful

my soul is broken
i need to be mended
by the lips that once said
i love you

i want a love so deep that we can't breathe without each other
a love that takes i love you
to never will i leave you
where words have consequences and contracts
a spell
only to be near you
those moments you gazed in my eyes i felt loved
our spirits danced
a dance of we and us
and when the us became i
and when the we became i
i alone was left
you alone were gone
never did i think it possible for us to be broken
not by those lips that swore love and fealty
not by those lips that gently kissed my body
not by those lips that promised the stars and moon
the distance
the vast incomprehensible lights in the sky
i stare and cry at the stars
that caused scars in me
through you
look to the sky
for as many stars there are shining towards me
that
there
is my pain
and my reasons to never give up
for as many stars that are in the sky
each is a reason i love you
a love so deep i could never understand
kiss me again slowly
tell me you don't feel a thing
so i can catch a star place it between your palms
and ask does it hurt you
to know i once held you
a glow unlike anything
a heat that mends my being
in essence
those stars you promised to are the reason i can't give up

Miguel Cruz

i secretly fear you
the first kiss we shared a warning
my beautiful storm
rip trees from roots
tear homes from people
flood our sinful city
but be the calm too
the hope of a better ending
a still sea with purple skies
be the first kiss i shared with you

i lick my fingers and turn the soft pages
each letter a mountain
the pain of writing words on a blank page
climb the letters
see the view
the beauty in you

Miguel Cruz

i forgot how you smile
all i see is tears
i remember your laughter
all i hear is jeers
forgotten or remembered
one thing is certain
all i want is you

my heart has threads
they hold my beating heart
although broken and tangled
there is one thread
you gave to me
made from your own
i hold onto this thread
i ask that you do too
blood from my heart spills
kiss my broken heart
let the silk from your needle
mend me and you

Miguel Cruz

to the stars that float at night
and the birds who sing and fly
to the girl whom i think at night
in remembrance let my light shine
let my love overcome you
love me
hold me sweet
take me to the skies
beautiful angel
i want to fly
i've felt it once and not again
a soft place
warm and full of delight
i pray to gods angels they bring me you
on my knees
you bend to me lord
and comfort me with your presence
a father looks upon his broken son
a son asks his father
for a girl
one girl
to come at night and love me
to write it out in destiny
for eternity
you and me
i pray my only star sees me
a broken dream made reality
i can never see a star shine as bright
and for that i will never give up
give in
just look up
look up to you lord
and my star that you created
for one day in my last breath
at your gates
i will say to you
thank you for my star
thank you for letting me love your most beautiful creation
thank you for everything
and to you my star
forgive me for not being strong enough to let go
for as long as you are in the skies
i will still have hope

dancing letters

our tongues dance when we speak
deeply thinking of things not thought of
i show you my love when i write
loyal to my red flower
you were taken by the wind
i stand strong realizing i'm too weak to go on
God himself carries me
like he did on the cross
our sins forgiven
our memories always known
he knew i would love you
in a way that would make him proud
a pure love
i pray for that
i already forgave you
for hurting me
the pain can be unbearable at times
but i remember that breath is still in you
that beat is for me
for as long as i have known you
i fell quite in love
red flower just come back to me
i will keep you safe

Miguel Cruz

i protect those i love
offering my life in their stead
when i'm in love
i would move mountains
grow gardens
give you the seas
our God created these things
these beautiful things
but nothing can compare to you

i have no words left
just know every thought is of you
memories hurt the worst
i still remember your smile
your laugh
and that time you cried because you felt overwhelmed and
misunderstood
seeing you cry made me realize i belong with you
i will cry with you
pray with you
and be everything you need
i'm the shoulder you cried on
and my shirt was your tissues
remember when i held you
know each day i think of that beautiful girl
my beautiful girl
who was in my arms when you needed me the most
remember when i held you
that's me

Miguel Cruz

look at the moon tonight
its slight sliver still makes it shine
i want to go up there
imagine if we made a picnic
i'd unfold a blanket
and bring your favorite fruit
you smile a smile that makes me float
your heart makes the stars jealous
hug me
it's cold up here
and that fire in your hair would keep me warm

we should live here
here things are perfect
what are your dreams
mine are right here
wait
where are you
why am i still here
if you are over there
i cry alone
but the thought of a picnic in the moon
is beautiful

i can't stay
this is goodbye
i'm sorry
this hurts me too
don't think i don't care deeply
those are things you said to me
those are the things that evidently broke me
i fell into broken pieces and forgave you
i waited
for you to fix me
i waited
for you to realize i'm worth it
i waited to see you fight
but now i'm hurt
i will not stay here broken
i will fight for us
and what little i have left
take it
take me
take every broken thing
cracks
tears
everything
take it for me
take it for you
let's be two beautiful broken people
i won't let them break you
but you break yourself
you are beautiful
wonderful
not perfect
but i don't expect you to be
those broken things inside you
i would kiss
i would mend
i will love
everything
anything
even if it means letting go
know that a special place is in my heart for you
little red flower
each petal you lose
i will love you for that too
just don't forget me
i will never forget you

dancing letters

i cried last night
looking at pictures of you
i danced alone in my room
i pretended it was with you
it was a sad night
but the thought of you holding my hand
took the sorrow away

Miguel Cruz

God made a flower for you
that's how special you are
a red rose
is what you are

dance with me
there is a room filled with candles
let's light each one
and make love
love on the floor
love towards our door
a love to adore
and from my core
the light will never die
you would never sigh
a simple lie
to ask why
in our bedroom
we speak truth
a simple lie
to ask why
did you break me
with each kiss
with each dance
just from your glance
dance with me
there is a room filled with candles

Miguel Cruz

a blue bird sings to me
as i sit on the edge of my window
who taught the bird the musical melodies
it's simply speaking
and i'm simply writing

simple truth of songs and words alike
maybe the bird needs a friend
or is it me
this bird knows my pain
and lives my dreams each day
i will always remember that blue bird
i just flew away

the room is empty
you sat there
and i'd lie here
the broken piano collected more dust
i play every broken key
this piano is different
it would play me
a king of fools
but the kings would be made to my fools
a foolish world
chaotic brilliance

Miguel Cruz

a red rose stirs my tea
tainting its nature
my nature to be
a rose flavored tea
in a golden mug
waiting to be drunk
only to be drunk
a drug to me
her name is

i haven't stopped falling
how can a man love a woman this deeply
the simple answer is
because you
but we don't live in a simple world
these black and white letters are simple enough
in a world of gray

a red apple hangs from a tree
it hangs for me
from seed to life
a beautiful thing
sweet bites to my delight
one day that apple will be mine
and with each bite i break you
till there is nothing left but the core
which i will throw away
in a place for you to be forgotten

Miguel Cruz

i did something last night
breaking a promise once made
i danced with another girl
she smiled and i stared everywhere
but at her
even in the music i sought you
it felt wrong
this is how we met
i never want to share that memory with anyone
our first dance changed me
i didn't know how broken i was till we met
with each spin i was lost in you further
my mind still spins to that night
spin with me again
get lost in me too

before you left
i treasured your worth
now i wander without
the x on my map guides me
i count stars and know my time is infinite
clawing my way through the sand
swimming across oceans
each day will be for my x

Miguel Cruz

28560207R00066

Made in the USA
Lexington, KY
16 January 2019